# Where Did the Sun Go?

Written by Karen Franco

Illustrated by Miranda Morrison-Jreige

"WHERE DID THE SUN GO?"
Copyright © 2018 by Karen Franco

ISBN 13: 978-1-73233-360-4
ISBN 10: 1-73233-360-2
Library of Congress PCN 2018956670

All Rights Reserved. No parts of this book may be reproduced or utilized in any form or by any means, electronic or mechanical, including photocopying, scanning, recording, or by any information storage and retrieval system now known or hereafter invented, without permission, in writing from the publisher.

To contact Karen Franco or order a copy of this book, please visit www.karenfrancobooks.com.

Published by
AMITY Publications
www.amitypublications.com

Printed in the United States of America

## Dedicated to...

My son, Jacob...every day you surprise and amaze
me by all that you accomplish.

**A Special Thank You to...**

Lindsey Slater, Meteorologist
WISN Channel 12 news in Milwaukee, WI,

for sharing her passion and knowledge of weather.

My Biggest Supporters...

My husband Chris, Jacob, and my dad, Jim Benko

Hi, I'm Jacob. Every morning, I look out my window to see if the sun is shining. When it is, I know I'm going to have a good day.

Today, when I look outside, I don't see the sun shining.
There are dark clouds in the sky and it is raining.
This makes me feel nervous.

I ask Mom, "Where did the sun go?"

Mom says, "The sun is hiding behind all the clouds. When the rain stops, the sun will come out again."

When I feel nervous, I start walking around the house and rocking back and forth. This helps me to calm down.

Today, when I look outside, I see gray sky and trees waving back and forth really fast. This makes me feel scared.

I ask Mom, "Where did the sun go?"

Mom says, "The sun is hiding behind all the clouds. When the rain stops, the sun will come out again."

When I feel scared, I say the same words over and over again. This helps me cope with my fears.

Today, when I look outside, I see lightning and hear thunder. This makes me feel unsafe.

I ask Mom, "Where did the sun go?"

Mom says, "The sun is hiding behind all the clouds. When the rain stops, the sun will come out again."

When I feel unsafe, Mom tells me everything is okay. Sometimes she gives me big bear hugs. The deep pressure feels good and helps me to feel better.

Mom watches the weather on the TV to check on the storm.
When the weather gets stormy, my behavior changes.
Sometimes I cry and run around the house yelling.

If the sky gets darker and the wind gets stronger,
we might have to go to a safe part of the house.

I sometimes feel confused and have a funny feeling inside. If I take deep breaths and count to twenty, that helps me calm down.

Mom makes sure I have my favorite books to read or puzzles to work on. If I'm busy playing, that helps me not think about the weather outside.

My dog, Bella, is always with me. She is very special and knows I get nervous during storms so stays close by to comfort me.

Sometimes Mom makes special books with pictures called "social stories." They explain step by step what is happening. These stories help me when I get scared or nervous or confused.

Mom will ask, "Do you remember what I told you about the rain?"

I do remember. She says rain helps the flowers and trees grow and makes the grass very green. But right now the sun is hiding behind the clouds. When the rain stops, the sun will come out again.

Stormy weather can be really scary but when I think about what Mom tells me, I feel better.

Look! The rain stopped and the sun is shining.
That makes me smile and feel very happy.
It's going to be a great day.

# Where Do Thunderstorms Come From?
by Meteorologist Lindsey Slater, WISN Channel 12, Milwaukee, WI

Thunderstorms start with energy from the sun as it begins to warm water droplets in the air. These droplets rise when they get warm but become colder and colder the higher they go. Then the droplets start to freeze and turn into thunderclouds. If there is enough water in the clouds and plenty of energy from the sun, a thunderstorm forms. When the energy is gone and there is no more water to rain out of the clouds, the thunderclouds get smaller and smaller. The rain turns into sprinkles. When the thunderstorm is over, the ground will be wet and there is a faint smell of freshness in the air.

# How the Weather Affects Children with Autism
*by Karen Franco*

As a parent of a child who has Autism, I know immediately when the weather is changing and the barometric pressure drops, Jacob's behaviors begin to change. There could be increased anxiety, impulsive behaviors and sensory issues that may occur. During these times it's important to try to keep his surroundings as calm as possible. I find that I need to talk more quietly, slowly and use very few words so I don't overwhelm him any more than he already is. Even a small distraction such as chewing a piece of gum or holding a toy such as a slinky could help to relieve the anxiety associated with the change in air pressure.*

In the sensory world, this process of distraction is called "grounding." When the anxiety starts, doing something "tangible" such as holding a key and running your finger on the edges or picking up something heavy like a paperweight. All these things will give the sensation of grounding. Jacob tends to hold the TV remote when he is feeling anxious. Why these activities work is that they help to distract Jacob from the anxious feelings. His brain can't be in two places at once.

*The Barometric Pressure is the weight of the overlying air pressing down on the earth. It can also be called "air pressure." Low barometric pressure means the overlying air is rising, whereas high pressure means the overlying air is sinking. High barometric pressure supports sunny, clear, and favorable weather conditions. Low barometric pressure promotes rainy and cloudy weather conditions. (Resource - Spirit of Autism, LLC)

## JUST THE END OF ANOTHER DAY!

**Other Books by Karen Franco:**

Just Hold My Hand
Jacob's Hoop
What Makes Bella Special?

www.ingramcontent.com/pod-product-compliance
Lightning Source LLC
Chambersburg PA
CBHW041541040426
42446CB00002B/186